T0129381

Midnight Madness

by

Jean Gabriel Aguilera

Order this book online at www.trafford.com
or email orders@trafford.com

Most Trafford titles are also available at major online book retailers.

© Copyright 2014 Jean Gabriel Aguilera.

Jean Aguilera
13920 Stirling Rd
SW Ranches, FL 33330
954-691-6674
iaguilera88@aol.com
Jeanaguilera3@gmail.com

Printed in the United States of America.

ISBN: 978-1-4907-4191-8 (sc)
ISBN: 978-1-4907-4190-1 (hc)
ISBN: 978-1-4907-4189-5 (e)

Library of Congress Control Number: 2014912567

Because of the dynamic nature of the Internet, any web addresses or links contained in
this book may have changed since publication and may no longer be valid. The views
expressed in this work are solely those of the author and do not necessarily reflect the
views of the publisher, and the publisher hereby disclaims any responsibility for them.

Any people depicted in stock imagery provided by Thinkstock are models,
and such images are being used for illustrative purposes only.
Certain stock imagery © Thinkstock.

Trafford rev. 07/14/2014

www.trafford.com
North America & international
toll-free: 1 888 232 4444 (USA & Canada)
fax: 812 355 4082

To my muse, Jolie
To my loving mother
and to my brother, Ivan, for
helping me achieve my dream.

4 31 55 AM

I came into town
From the uncomfortable sound
That gave way to the sea
Drowning the mysterious me
Who there? Stood there?
A silhouette that formed everywhere
Nonsense becomes some sense
Burning heavy on the mind of past tense
Changing shapes, unrecognizable to the ordinary eye
I bleed untold sadness to the individual sky
Speaking names I only heard from stories
And walking on sand that only stuck me with worries
How much? Too much?
Can the wicked have their touch?
On all the clouds that are born
Does your future get torn?
I gave away a piece of peace
To have myself a blooming day to cease
Dirty and undertaken, I sample new lips
Wrong and mistaken, I'm the bully of good kids
Singing songs that break the breathing heart
Because I'm not satisfied with what I came to start
No suitable fit for arms to keep
I drink the night so I may sleep
Unholy with no glory, dancing with loneliness
Lies my unconscious mind under hopelessness

6_10

I saw the sun form in the sky
Birds grew to learn how to fly
But shot down by cannons
That I heard coming from beyond
The sea that we all came to free
Cities scream loud and wrong
Attention. Attention. Attention.
People look with such desire
And there's a fire that burns deep to inspire
To silence the violence that brings ignorance
A mirror on the floor
But no eyes want to look down
To see the chaos and more
That breathes inside and breeds destruction
Only leaving tears that fall out of the earth
Dreams wake and dollars give change
I chose tomorrow over today
Just to smile for a while and remember the page
That I held in my hand when I was six or ten
God knew where I was back then
But I took a ship to space to see if I could live again
Started skiing to maybe buy a friend
Lost in mysteries with no solution
Sleep is a battle that is deprivation
I fight with tooth and nail for open eyes
I saw a sun form up in the skies

Blue

I blue back to you
In hopes to find true
That if I could dream through
Then maybe you could too
But the harder I blue
No plant ever grew
And truth is I knew
My leaves already flew
I whisper in tantalizing rue
Of the path I wish I drew
Though it's nothing to say I'm blue
Keep the love I blue to you

A Raining Silhouette

A shadow shuffles itself through the pouring rain
Confiscating tiny particles of cherished streams
I have seen this before; this shadow galore
Running down chimneys; stuffing its hole
Puddles of puss constricting a fuss
Yearning for a compelling alignment
Of the sun and the moon
To lay on the same afternoon
But this shadow does shuffle
And often it muffles
All of the beloved transitions
We once came to hold
Between our vivid, pumping compassion
So as this shadow comes shuffling
I will hold my chest with buoyancy
For an angel is behind me
And her light does not abate
Upon a shadow that waits

Another Rather Lovely Thing

The skies chandelier covers paradise
The cool tear drops of a worn out cloud
Showers over everything
A voice is heard
Over the loud roars of wind
I can't think of a single thought
Of how to flow through your eyes
But it's nothing now
He holds your hand in the kindest way
And I am nothing now
I'll hold your heart in the greatest way
You're just another rather lovely thing

Everywhere

You're everywhere
Like my shadow from there to here
You surround my entire frontier
Every painting on the wall
Every white flower that has grown tall
You're everywhere
Each song I hear sings your name
Every melody is yours to claim
Every motion picture shows your face
I catch your beauty and all your grace
You're everywhere
All the stars have your eyes
And I've lost count in all my tries
Every breeze brings in your smile
I can't help but to dream for a while
You're everywhere
Every book I come to read
Every breath I come to need
Every sight that there's to see
Every strand of gold that falls unto me
You *are* everywhere
And even though at times
It feels like misery
I wouldn't dare change my scenery
Because I wouldn't know what to do
If I did not have you

Fall

Motion sickness from all the pretend
Rewind the tapes so I can hear it again
I saw the moon cash out its shine
I'm wasted in space asking for time
Pale blue frame
It cripples to think you aren't the same
I'm out of breath before I start
If I chew out my thoughts maybe I wont fall apart
Rain drips from my face
The trophy seems far but I'm still in this race
I'll seek out the frontier
Have I dried off or am I still here?
Daydreams bring out the sun
Because nothing ever feels like its done
I fall through the air and it keeps me from seeing the ground
Pushing my hands towards the clouds I wont make a sound
Hope may be wild
To say the least
But I'll save it just to see
Whatever these days may bring for me

Fireworks

I see fireworks
And I think of us
Because we're fire that works
We are fire that burns
Our flames can't be extinguished
And our light can't be diminished
I see fireworks
And I think of us
For both our signs ignite our hearts
With love thundering down
You have set this dark forest of mine ablaze
To free me from the tormenting haze
The rain may pour but our fire cannot be tamed
It runs wild through the stars that are yet to be named
This fire reflects from your eyes to mine
And scorches through our souls
I see fireworks
And I think of us
Because we the paint the sky with beauty
And both of us together is truly a sight to see

Gardinias

This flower I keep
I water daily
It never comes to seep
And stays strong eternally
The thought of it fading
Is simply impossible
There's only room for elevating
Because I know how I'm capable
To stay this way
Each and every coming day
But this flower may belong to a different garden
Keeping my head up just seems like a burden
It's a task
To wear a different mask
But I heard someone say;
"Never say never."
So I'll look ahead
For a better kind of weather
And keep watering this flower
Because my love grows hour after hour

Hopes Window

Where the window lies
Is a new surprise
Towards the coldest frontier
Next to the oldest chandelier
I see three sets of stars
Shining against the earth
Reminding me of the evenings glow
Where lovers grow
Inside the winds blow
Beside a strangers eye
From where dreamers go
These three little stars
Each one shooting a massive trail
Of hope and faith to ones understanding
Of fear and fret to ones undermining
I cradle a song
To never again long
The lips of a soul I came to know
Where this window does lie
I meet the sky

If I Knew

Guide me in circles
Around the tree and into the bank
Beyond the fields
So I may know where I rank
These dandelions pour towards the east
Where I found love to tame the beast
But can I remain standing forever?
My eyes are weary from searching a four-leaf clover
I broke the bay just to reach yesterday
Because that's where I am and that's where I'll stay
To live on a vicious cycle around and about
Prove the earth that I can't live without
You slowly begin to fade from me
And I am shattered beyond normal eyes can see
I smile crookedly just to see you shine
Because happiness has never been a friend of mine
If I knew what to say when you catch my eyes
Then I would speak broken tuned lies
For I can't reveal the truth that paints you
It's too much pain to pass through
If I knew how to reach new plains
That would ease your troubles without any rains
I would form a new a new living ground
If I knew how to change my sound

Jealousy

Daggers dig through my stomach
In and out I muscle about
Because what right do I have?
To show green on my side
I drink heavy thoughts
As my eyes begin to rot
Hand on hand, you have what I wish I had
Jealousy can drive a man mad
My mouth is dry
With my back towards the sky
Pulled hair covers the floor
I'm sure I can take much more
Lip on lip crumbles my town
Jealousy can put a man down
I lose my breathing
As the waves come crashing
This current shakes my heart
Drags and pulls me apart
Dress me up to hide my face
I fiddle to stay in place
Skin on skin rattles my brain
Jealousy can turn a man insane

Leap

Tip the scale and feel the sudden rush
There are words to inhale, so allow them to gush
I looked towards a cloud
And I swear I saw silver
I smiled in a way
That I knew it would be sooner
To catch the pitchers eye
What a disguised blessing from the sky
I focus on this tunnels exit
Because I feel what comes with it
Something static that is electric
To make me ecstatic along with collective
A leap towards faith is all that's left to do
And breathe in what I know is true
A painting can change its wall
And a ceiling that crumbles to fall
May seem disastrous at first sight
But makes way for an everlasting light

Mamihlapinatapai

My thoughts burst like bubbles
Releasing all my troubles
It's a struggle to keep my instincts away
To not form a shell and go astray
Because how much longer can I keep my eyes up?
Without any fortune or good luck
I shake my head as to dwindle my thoughts
But they haunt me to send my brain to rot
I stand under the ocean
Just to escape any emotion
But I can't let you slip through my fingers
Everything we've shared still lingers
We're electric to the touch
I see it when you blush
Trapped is everything we look for
I'm still chasing you through that door
I know you see what I see in you and me
To fight the urge is to defy gravity
But we stand far apart
Knowing what lies in our heart

Name

Silent pillars of sand
Storm in a sudden sound
Sucking and searching for simple silhouettes
Seeing, saving, slaving
I chant her name
A dozen times
Constant remorse to the weary change
I grow plastic wings
Singing sonnets that may never grow
Burning through piles of snow
I chant her name
A dozen times
And clear my thoughts
Of thoughtless tries
Wounded but grateful of a forgotten road
I tear down the walls
And bathe in cement just to find my heart
In sweet dusk I cover the floor
Scream in laughter on all fours
And swallow the dust once more
Dancing in a midnight flame
I chant her name
A single name
A million times

She

She is breath
She is the breeze
Of a soft summer day
She is the ocean
Clear and full of wonders
She is the wind
That sings sweetly to my blessed soul
She is brighter than the stars
And to gaze upon her
Is far beyond greater than great
Than to gaze at the stars
Because to have her
The universe needs no stars
No sun, no moon
She is all
She is light
She is the essence of beauty itself
And to capture that in only one look
Is simply and utterly impossible
She is a symphony and she is peace
She is only what your dreams can dream of
She smiles a smile
That will lift you off your feet
She is mother to all who she loves
She is a blessing to all who she loves
A guardian angel
She is life

Solace

Crippled by simplicity
Under new afternoons that feel old
But if I knew where this yellow brick will take me
Would I want to be told?
You were an itch that turned into a rash
That distracts me from stability
And directs me to crash
Unto misery and pure iniquity
I pray for an antidote or maybe the opposite
Because really a taste is all I want from you
To indulge in the sweetness you deposit
From the emotions that seep through
But denial shouts its name
These can't be the reasons I hold on
There must be more in to why I came
Or is it really all just for fun?
Denial shouts with no meaning
Intentionally, my intentions are unfair
My skin is cold from the past
That's still breathing and lingering
That leaves a sense of sadness in the air
I'm lost in the forest of my mind
To never find solace with whatever I find

Solitude

At star gaze through a maze
Of wonders and grace
I see what may be
And what might have been
Images of us as we
In ways that I've never seen
But the shed of fear
Crosses my atmosphere
To spawn doubt in and out
Through the heart I was positive about
With shelters and walls
I lean so as not to fall
And feel the cold cement floor
As my happiness rushes though the door
But as I star gaze in this maze of mine
Of the purpose I chase through endless time
I capture the moonlight and it's form
That comforts me in every coming storm
I build her name out of ice and snow
And hold her with love to never let go
Solitude.
An everlasting wave that drowns my mind and soul
To wither me in complete control

Sonnet 5

She enters in warmth and I can't complain
I wallow in desperation for another time
She sings words that melt in my brain
And gifts me care that's too sublime
I am always compelled when she comes to me
With embracing arms, she has her way
I would swim against the sea
Just so I may see her another day
But this consumption is not well
And I mustn't take more of her delight
For her glittering clouds will bring a grim bell
To never again give me light
I can't control my shaking eyes
When she brings around her soothing skies

Sonnet 6

A castle in the sea and people running high
Some sunny rays shooting through
With emotions on the curve of the sky
And waves of warmth coming from you
Birds sing and rainbows form
Trees have grown off of the side of my bed
This different dimension is away from the storm
This different dimension is in my head
But nothing is here for me to find
This dimension is far but close to me
The uncomforting veracity I must leave behind
To never contain what I always see
These eyes of mine blink from ejection
These hands of mine concentrate in contemplation

Sonnet 7

A summer kiss has gone dry
When midnight struck I heard the sun
I have met the devils eye
So I could see what can be done
Chains have grown where I lay
To keep me far apart from light
And clouds of despair come to say
That this time and place is never right
But this precious jewel is far too long
It is true what these thoughts have thought
I am the bird with the same old song
Chanting the soul that can not be forgot
An embellished dream comes to me
With pillars of beam that I will never see

Sonnet 8

The motion is set on high
I wonder with by blunder
Towards the green colored sky
That sets in an astonishing thunder
With the wind singing a symphony
And a soothing eruption taking control
With the clouds creating mystery
The young moon embraces my soul
But the spinning begins faster than light
Corrupting the world that dances with me
I tremble with worry and stumble in fright
For these shadows of hell are all I can see
A heavy wave comes to take me away
Troubled bricks fall my way

Sonnet 9

A whisper is never heard
Kindness is a favorable aspect for the weak
Endurance just sounds absurd
Though I may never last if we don't speak
My growing warmth for you
Grows beyond my mind
I wish to catch the pedal that flows through
That sings in motions every soul tries to find
But my attempts have tired my bones
And my contemplation to leave is at a higher state
I cannot keep a straight walk with endless moans
Yet the desired desire will never disintegrate
The days are nights I hope to forget
The smiles and sun dances I can never regret

Sonnet 10

What must be done is always a torment
For just once in a season
I wish for something different
A better source a joyful reason
A place where we can both roam
An afternoon we can both share
Words of laughter we don't need to own
And days of kindness we can all declare
But what must be done must be done
It's a compelling hell in disguise
The laughter and smiles are all gone
All that is left is a side to despise
I can't keep the old house with me
There is a shattering sadness with every dying tree

Sonnet 11

Drowning the faces I saw yesterday
For tomorrow asks more than time
Open but lost in this wondering bay
Chanting songs that have a familiar chime
I could carry the weight that the sky drops
With every hour that is given to me
I can keep my rhythm after the tune stops
And walk on grounds no one can see
But reality out runs my expectation
For what I seek sleeps somewhere unknown
Smiling with every ounce of compassion
I long to see what isn't heard or shown
Broken and heavy, my knees do feel weak
As the pain splatters, I'll turn my cheek

Spring

Broken stars burn slow
I can barely breathe whenever they glow
Mark my heavy eyes
I just need spring to cover my skies
I'm lost inside this storm
Spilling my words but nothing takes form
Nightmares come dressed as dreams
Builds me a sun that doesn't shower its beam
Help me shut off my brain
Just for a day to maybe stay sane
I'll cover my face
So no one can see that I'm out of place
Can you push back the demons
That settle themselves around me?
Hold open a window
When there's no door left to see
Can you push back the demons
That break me in two?
Hold my body
When I can't push myself through
And if a should go bad
Would you still keep me close?
I have my tendencies to drown
Just know you're my light when it all turns black

Stay Awake

Stay awake,
And I'll steal you the moon
Open your eyes
To see that these dreams come soon
I know it's not over
Because I can feel through the walls
Keep up your eyelids
And respond to the calls
That the sky gives you and I
To hold onto the reason why
My eyes are heavy but I keep them alive
Because with sleep it won't survive
Pull up the curtains
And push in the sun
So that we may keep the surface
Because this story's not done
Drink in the melodies
That provide you with glee
Turn off the darkness
And hold onto me
I know it's a leap
To not fall asleep
But with the stars aligning towards you
I'll stay awake
Because I know you're awake too

Winter

I shiver from east to west
Caught on the strip with a hand on my chest
My eyes begin to blur
Drunk on the thought, before I begin to pour
I'm not meant for this town
I spin out of place when I hit the ground
Have my worn smile for good
I've lost cause for what it stood
Is there a reason that's lost?
Blank on the screen, that buried my cost
Paint me my heart
It's what you own from finish to start
Piles on my bones and I'm spent, I can't keep my mind clear
Remember my imprints on your skin while you lay near
Have your share plate of me
Feel what you can't see
From all that I have
Left and right on my soul
From all that I have
Left tonight on my floor
Nothings left on my side
Nothing is ever on my side

Your Voice

Your voice
It's serenity at its best
Just by the sound
I can feel the beat in my chest
When there is struggle
And all I see is night
Your regal voice
Shows me the light
Because when the day gets blurry
And I start to worry
Your voice is there
To steady my hands
To bring me back from the sea
That swallows me whole
And drowns every part of me
Your voice
Brings the calm without the storm
No sadness can ever form
From your voice
Because your voice
That sentimental
Instrumental
Heartwarming voice
Exorcises my demons
And unburdens my mind
That voice alone
Your voice
Brings the sun from the moon
And I know we're coming soon

Boardwalk

Crashing over bottles
Cause I can
For me, for my heart
Clear my throat
And climb on my back
To see from the start
Close my eyes
And I just hope
That a wish can be heard
From a great length
Andwhen I breathe
I remember the smiles that you bring
So make your choice quick
Please don
Gold never comes in for free
I mumble counting sheep
Under my bed
Realizing,
The moon isn
To capture mywicked soul
Ofwhich I long to let go
For something worth knowing
Arapture to have growing
Coupled with the broken paragraphs
That lead to a brighter ending
But one that I know I could never have
Seeing is believing
And dreaming is living
But this dreaming is leaving

Lost Thoughts on Coffee Breaks

Mute the sound of winter
Slingshot to the east side
The frontier speaks alone
And you shove through
Around and away
It
For my crooked bones
Something beneath my soul
Takes complete control
Bringing symphonies of shame
For my broken heart
Something behind my head
Makes your lips turn red
And I can
The root of regret
The chaos of sleep
For you sir!
The crust on the floor
Yes you sir
Beating for more
So you sir!
Your defensive words
Will blind he dear mind
For you sir
Your egotistic ways
Will just leave her behind
Now you sir
The morning has come
Andmadness draws nigh
Because you sir
Are the cold particles in the sky

Silver Plate

I get cold
My body shakes for the sun
But I'm told
That shaking resolves to more fun
So move me in ways
That no other soul can explain
Bleed your words
Leave your mark on the side of my brain
Grow wide on my skin
Bend your head and breathe
You say that you're falling away
But I can't catch you
Move down and leave
My head spins out of control
You did your job, now goodbye
You don't learn
My hands are stained from the red
But your eyes burn
Your nuisance gets heavy on my head
I'll turn you around
But you can't seem to forget
And when you get down
I'll enjoy the plate that you set
Melt my eyelids
Job well done hun, so goodbye

Whirlwind in the Indigo

I move inside the blender
My heart beats faster as I move
And I can't remember
Why I ever came
So I start to slow down
I begin to chew my words right
And I hope I found
What I've been waiting for
And the air flows so well
As you walk towards the sun
And my eyes can't tell
What they have won
You in the light
What a gorgeous sight
I know you've seen better years
I know time gets hard
But I really do wish
You end up here
And fall asleep between my arms
I walk in steady
Spilling all that's on my mind
But I start to choke up
Because you might not have the time
So I walk back out
Into the cold breeze I once knew
I hear a hard knock
I'm hoping that it's you
But you know I like
The silly words that come out to dance

And I know I might
Never have a chance
I look up just like before
Asking, "Send me more!"
I know you've seen better years
I know time gets hard
But I really do wish
You end up here
And fall asleep between my arms